V&A Pattern
Chinese Textiles

V&A Publishing

V&A Pattern

Chinese Textiles

First published by V&A Publishing, 2010
V&A Publishing
Victoria and Albert Museum
South Kensington
London SW7 2RL

ISBN 978 1 85177 622 1
Library of Congress Control Number 2010925923

10 9 8 7 6 5 4 3 2 1
2014 2013 2012 2011 2010

A catalogue record for this book is available
from the British Library.

Series Art Direction: Rose
Design: TurnbullGrey www.turnbullgrey.co.uk

Front cover (A):
Dragon robe, embroidery on silk
China, *c.*1736–96 (V&A: T.197–1948, Vuilleumier Collection, purchased with the assistance of The Art Fund)
Pages 2–3 (B):
Dragon robe, woven silk tapestry
China, early 19th century (V&A: T.756–1950)
Page 6 (C):
Theatrical costume, embroidery on silk
China, early 20th century (V&A: T.45–1933, Given by Mr Paul King, through the Art Fund)
Page 11 (D):
Lengths of patterned silk
China, *c.*1960–65 (V&A: FE.53-56–1999, Given by Ellen Johnston Laing)
Pages 78–9 (E):
Dragon robe, woven silk tapestry
China, 1736–1820 (V&A: T.189–1948, Vuilleumier Collection, purchased with the assistance of The Art Fund)

Letters (in brackets) refer to the file name of the
images on the accompanying disc.

Printed in China

V&A Publishing
Victoria and Albert Museum
South Kensington
London SW7 2RL
www.vandabooks.com

V&A Pattern

Each *V&A Pattern* book is an introduction to the Victoria and Albert Museum's extraordinarily diverse collection. The museum has more than three million designs for textiles, decorations, wallpapers and prints; some well-known, others less so. This series explores pattern-making in all its forms, across the world and through the centuries. The books are intended to be both beautiful and useful – showing patterns to enjoy in their own right and as inspiration for new design.

V&A Pattern presents the greatest names and styles in design, while also highlighting the work of anonymous draughtsmen and designers, often working unacknowledged in workshops, studios and factories, and responsible for designs of aesthetic originality and technical virtuosity. Many of the most interesting and imaginative designs are seen too rarely. *V&A Pattern* gathers details from our best objects and hidden treasures from pattern books, swatch books, company archives, design records and catalogues to form a fascinating introduction to the variety and beauty of pattern at the V&A.

The compact disc at the back of each book invites you to appreciate the ingenuity of the designs, and the endless possibilities for their application. To use the images professionally, you need permission from V&A Images, as the V&A controls – on behalf of others – the rights held in its books and CD-Roms. *V&A Pattern* can only ever be a tiny selection of the designs available at www.vandaimages.com. We see requests to use images as an opportunity to help us to develop and improve our licensing programme – and for us to let you know about images you may not have found elsewhere.

Chinese Textiles
Yueh-Siang Chang

Chinese silk textiles have a long and prestigious history with examples traceable to the late Neolithic period (*c.*3000–2000 BC). Although silk was not unique to China, silkworm domestication was a preciously guarded secret that enabled the Chinese to produce fine, lustrous, unbroken filaments that were in turn transformed into cloth.

As weaving technology progressed, looms were used to create textiles with increasingly complex and intricate patterns. Early Chinese textile designs tend to have simple geometric patterns or basic shapes and lines, owing to the relative simplicity of early looms. Other shapes and repeat patterns developed later as a result of advances in technology and the exchange of ideas with foreigners. For example, the swastika motif was introduced to China in about 250 BC, around the same time as Buddhism. Such patterns of geometric shapes and lines became characteristic of Chinese design: a repeated pattern of interweaving lines or circular shapes now symbolizing infinity or eternity (plate 22). Soon after, the development of embroidery would lead to more sophisticated decoration.

Chinese textiles, particularly those made for clothing, often feature talismanic and auspicious symbols and sometimes religious motifs. The Buddhist 'endless knot' (plate 17) and Taoism's *taiji* diagram, more commonly known as the *yin-yang* disc (plates 25 and 26), are particularly popular. By adorning oneself with such symbols, woven or embroidered into repeat patterns, the wearer may have hoped to receive good fortune or protection against evil.

Although silk was commonly worn even among people of lower status, the ruling classes asserted their superiority by controlling the colours and designs worn by the civilian population. Sun and moon motifs were reserved for royal use as early as the Warring States period (476–221 BC). Although dragons and phoenixes were popular in folk art, certain specific depictions, such as a dragon bearing five claws, were part of the Twelve Imperial Insignia, reserved exclusively for imperial use. By the time of the Qing Dynasty (1644–1911), dragons had become synonymous with imperial rank in clothing and accessories and appeared on most robes produced for royals and high-ranking princes and officials.

Despite sumptuary regulations, civilians could still wear garments decorated with a wealth of symbols and motifs, often derived from nature, landscapes and even calligraphy. Part of the charm of Chinese imagery is its use of objects to represent a concept; such pictorial codes offer infinite sources of inspiration for textile patterns. For example, flowers and fruit depict noble qualities because their natural characteristics are considered worthy of emulation; bamboo, a plant that rarely bends, symbolizes personal strength; the attractive flower of the peony indicates elegance and purity of character; the fruitfulness of the pomegranate hints at the abundance of progeny. Sometimes objects or animals derive their symbolic meaning from being identical in pronunciation to an auspicious word: bats for luck (*fu*), deers for success in professional prospects (*lu*). Such animals may then be paired with embellished Chinese script characters to make their message explicit: textiles that feature bats and the character for longevity (*shou*) denote a long life with good luck; bats coupled with the *xi* ('double happiness') character communicates a wish for happiness and good fortune, primarily in the context of a wedding.

Chinese silks and their imagery captured the imagination of foreigners as early as 200 BC when they were first used outside Chinese domains as diplomatic gifts. Traditional floral and auspicious symbols were later adapted to foreign tastes, as is apparent in textiles woven, painted or embroidered for export, particularly those produced in the seventeenth and eighteenth centuries. Fruit and flowers not native to China, such as the palm, came to be featured on some silks. Floral motifs on export textiles differ in style from conventional Chinese designs of trellises and scrolls, with those decorating painted textiles depicted with botanical realism, emulating the natural history drawings so popular with Europeans.

The majority of symbols that appear on Chinese textiles have evolved over centuries, even millennia, to form the vocabulary of traditional Chinese imagery. From 1910 to the late 1930s, however, a new Chinese republic replaced centuries of dynastic rule, and began a process of modernization that would see tradition overthrown in favour of modernity. Textile patterns began to reflect more Western aesthetics, including Art Deco patterns and simple Modernist lines. When the Communists came to power in 1949, the mass production of textiles came to represent the People's Republic of China's industrial and technological capacity. In addition to silk, new cotton and synthetic fabrics became commonplace while improved machinery standardized weaving and printing, allowing for more complex repeat patterns. In some instances, textiles became tools of propaganda, with brightly patterned fabrics echoing Mao's cry to 'Let a Hundred Flowers Bloom!' In 1995, in a tongue-in-cheek play on communist China's participation in the twentieth-century global fashion economy, designer Vivienne Tam adorned her runway collection with the iconic image of Chairman Mao, who had advocated that Chinese people abandon 'old ideas, old culture, old customs and old habits'.

1
Fragment, silk damask
China, 14th–16th century (V&A: 7052–1860, Bock Collection)

2
Table frontal, embroidery on silk
China, 1670–1730 (V&A: T.37–1911)

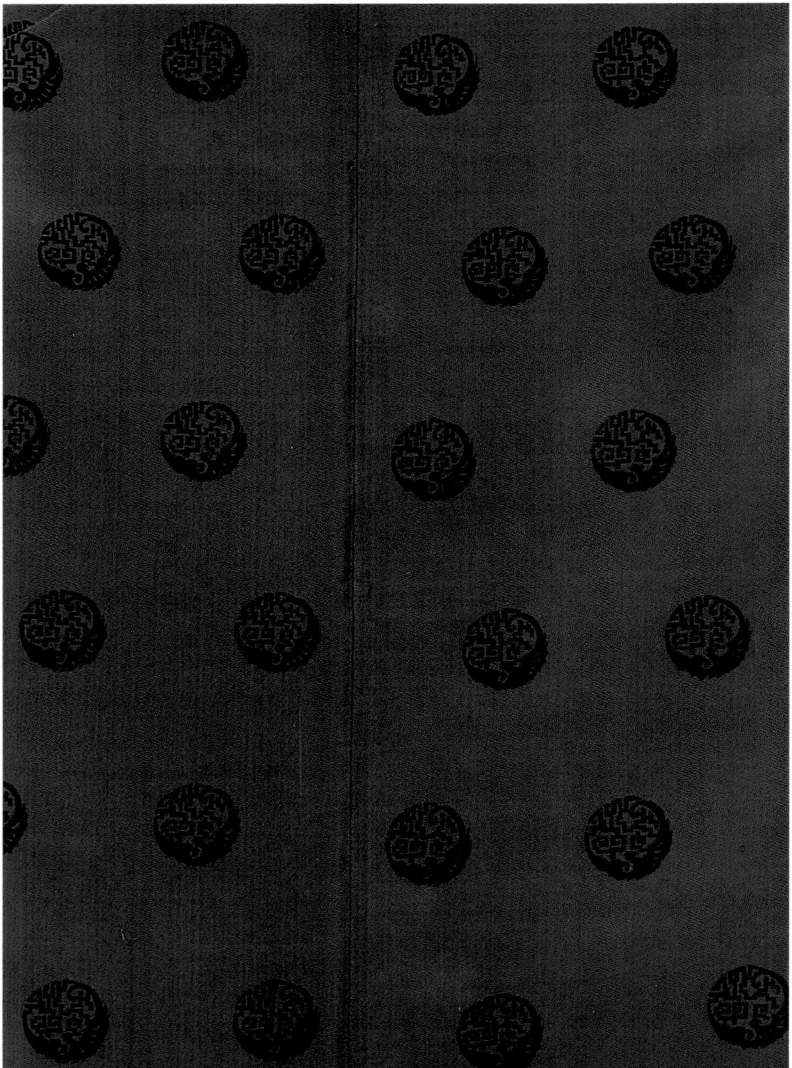

3
Robe, silk velvet
China, 20th century (V&A: FE.125–1983, Addis Bequest)

4
Panel, embroidery on silk
China, 19th century (V&A: 1607A–1901)

5
Fragment, woven silk
China, 19th century (V&A: T.361A–1910, Given by Lady Wilson)

6
Marriage robe, woven silk tapestry
China, 19th century (V&A: T.223–1948)

7
Buddhist thangka, embroidery on silk
China, 1777 (V&A: T.31–1950)

8
Woman's robe, embroidery on silk
China, 1850–61 (V&A: T.173–1961)

9
Woman's jacket, silk velvet
Hong Kong, *c.*1969 (V&A: FE.45–1997, Given by Mrs Victoria Dicks)

10
Woman's robe, embroidery on silk
China, 1870–1911 (V&A: T.231–1948, Vuilleumier Collection, purchased with the assistance of The Art Fund)

11
Woman's robe, embroidery on silk with applied coral and seed pearls
China, 1800–1911 (V&A: T.253–1967)

12
Curtain from a wedding palanquin, embroidery on silk
China, late 19th–early 20th century (V&A: T.44F–1952, Given by Sir Steven Runciman)

13
Robe, woven silk tapestry
China, early 17th century (V&A: FE.41–1985, Purchased with a grant donated by Lady Garner)

14
Woman's skirt, embroidery on silk
China, late 19th–early 20th century (V&A: FE.12–1980)

15
Woman's robe, embroidery on silk
China, late 19th century (V&A: T.230–1948, Vuilleumier Collection, purchased with the assistance of The Art Fund)

16
Sleeve band, embroidery on silk
China, 19th century (V&A: Circ.807–1912)

17
Length of silk gauze
China, 1880–1930 (V&A: FE.114–1983, Addis Bequest)

18
Length of woven silk
China, 19th–20th century (V&A: FE.110–1983, Addis Bequest)

19
Length of woven silk
China, 19th–20th century (V&A: FE.134–1983, Addis Bequest)

20
Length of silk brocade
China, *c.*1915 (V&A: T.52–1915, Given by TB Clarke–Thornhill)

21
Robe for a temple statue, silk brocade
China, cyclical date equivalent to 1791 or 1851 (V&A: T.752–1950)

22
Dragon robe, woven silk tapestry
China, 1780–1850 (V&A: T.199–1948, Vuilleumier Collection, purchased with the assistance of The Art Fund)

23
Rank badge, silk embroidery
China, 18th–19th century (V&A: T.140–1948, Vuilleumier Collection, purchased with the assistance of The Art Fund)

24
Rank badge, embroidery on silk
China, late 18th–early 19th century (V&A: T.164–1965)

25
Taoist priest's robe, embroidery on silk
China, 18th century (V&A: 1620–1901)

26
Girl's jacket, resist-dyed cotton
China, early 20th century (V&A: T.234–1966)

27
Buddhist textile picture, woven silk
China, 1740–1800 (V&A: T.97–1966)

28
Woman's robe, embroidery on silk
China, 19th century (V&A: T.209–1948, Vuilleumier Collection, purchased with the assistance of The Art Fund)

29
Length of silk damask
China (for the export market), *c.*1850 (V&A: AP.413:2)

30
Fragment, silk damask
China, 16th–18th century (V&A: 1404–1899)

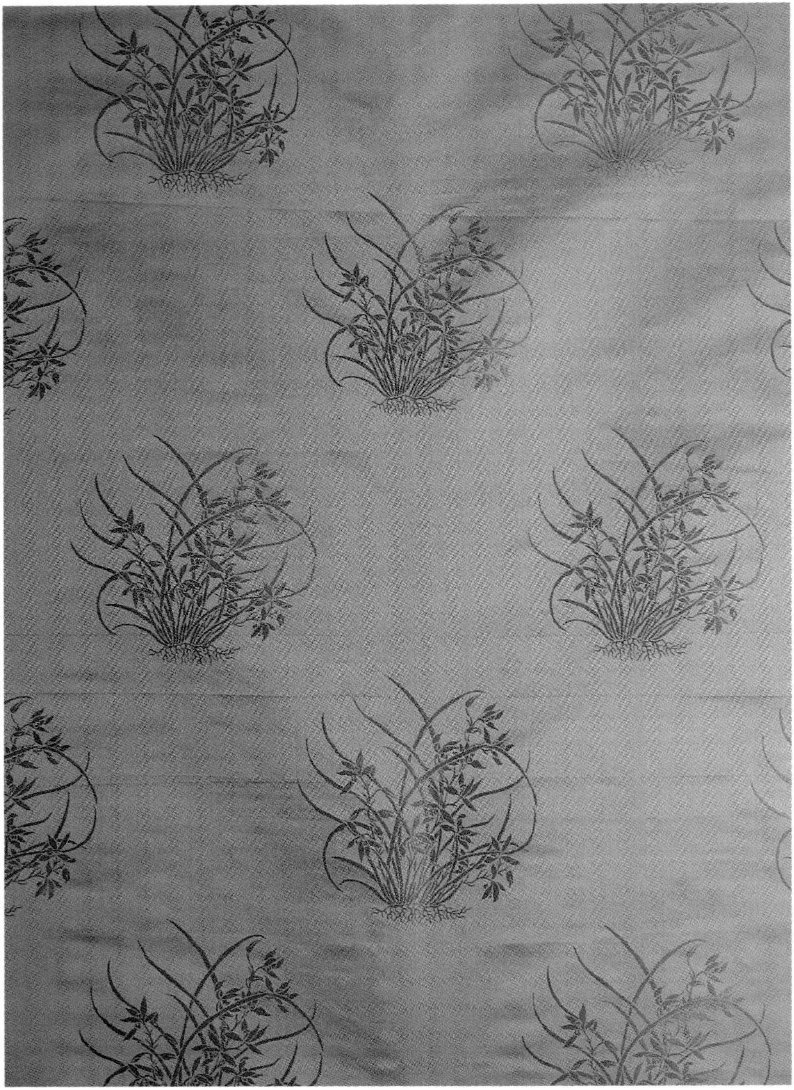

31
Length of silk damask
China, late 19th–early 20th century (V&A: T.276–1962)

32
Length of silk gauze
China, 1880–1930 (V&A: FE.99–1983, Addis Bequest)

33
Fragment, woven silk
China, 19th century (V&A: T.361D–1910, Given by Lady Wilson)

34
Fragment, woven silk
China, 13th–17th century (V&A: T.198–1909)

35
Man's robe, silk velvet
China, 20th century (V&A: FE.126–1983, Addis Bequest)

36
Curtain, embroidery on ramie
China, 1830–40 (V&A: FE.150–1983, Given by Mrs Perkins H. Bailey)

37
Woman's jacket, embroidery on silk
China, 19th–20th century (V&A: T.53–1970, Bequeathed by Dame Ada MacNaghten)

38
Woman's robe, embroidery on gauze silk
China, mid 19th century (V&A: T.32–1950)

39
Textile cover, embroidery on silk
China, 1900–30 (V&A: FE.117–1974, Given by Joan Evans)

40
Woman's robe, embroidery on silk
China, early to mid 19th century (V&A: T.52–1970, Bequeathed by Dame Ada MacNaghten)

41
Woman's robe, embroidery on silk
China, 19th century (V&A: T.26–1958)

42
Woman's jacket, embroidery on silk
China, late 19th century (V&A: T.2–1957)

43
Woman's robe, embroidery on silk
China, late 17th–18th century (V&A: T.184–1948, Vuilleumier Collection, purchased with the assistance of The Art Fund)

44
Girl's surcoat, embroidery on silk
China, early 20th century (V&A: T.110–1964)

45
Sleeve band, embroidery on silk
China, 19th century (V&A: Circ.787–1912)

46
Length of silk velvet
China, 17th–18th century (V&A: FE.9–1980)

47
Length of silk damask
China (for the export market), *c.*1850 (V&A: AP.413:3)

48
Length of silk damask
China (for the export market), *c.*1850 (V&A: AP.412:3)

49
Panel, painted silk
China (for the export market), *c.*1810 (V&A: T.122–1933)

50
Length of painted silk
China (for the export market), late 18th century (V&A: T.110–1926)

51
Panel, painted silk
Guangzhou, China (for the export market), 1760–1800 (V&A: T.3–1948)

52
Length of painted silk
China (for the export market), *c.*1770–80 (V&A: T.121–1933, Deedes Gift)

53
Panel, painted silk
China (for the export market), *c.*1780 (V&A: T.131–1925)

54
Quilt, painted silk gauze
China (for the export market), *c.*1800–10 (V&A: T.119–1949, Munro Gift)

55
Bedspread, embroidery on silk
China (for the export market), *c.*1770–90 (V&A: T.387–1970, Given by Mr and Mrs GHG Norman)

56
Bed cover, embroidery on satin silk
China (for the export market), *c.*1760–70 (V&A: FE.12–2004, Purchased with the support of the Friends of the V&A)

57
Men's robe, pattern-woven silk
China, 1920–50 (V&A: FE.29–1995, Garrett Collection, Purchased with the support of the Friends of the V&A)

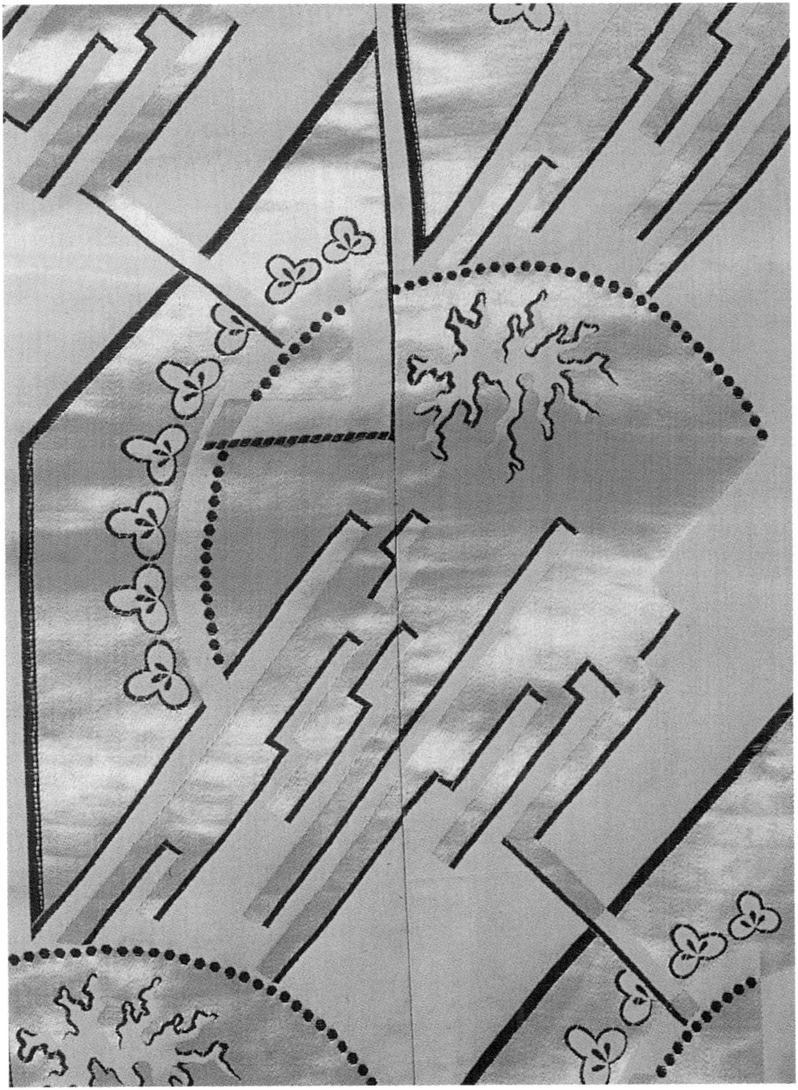

58
Woman's jacket, silk
Shanghai, China, *c.*1915 (V&A: FE.61–1995, Given by Mrs B. Roney)

59
Length of silk velvet
China, 1900–20 (V&A: FE.106–1983, Addis Bequest)

60
Woman's jacket, silk
Shanghai, China, *c.*1915 (V&A: FE.64–1997, Given by Mrs B. Roney)

61
Length of printed cotton
China, *c.*1978 (V&A: FE.14–1994, Given by Clio Whittaker)

62
Length of printed cotton
China, *c.*1978 (V&A: FE.15–1994, Given by Clio Whittaker)

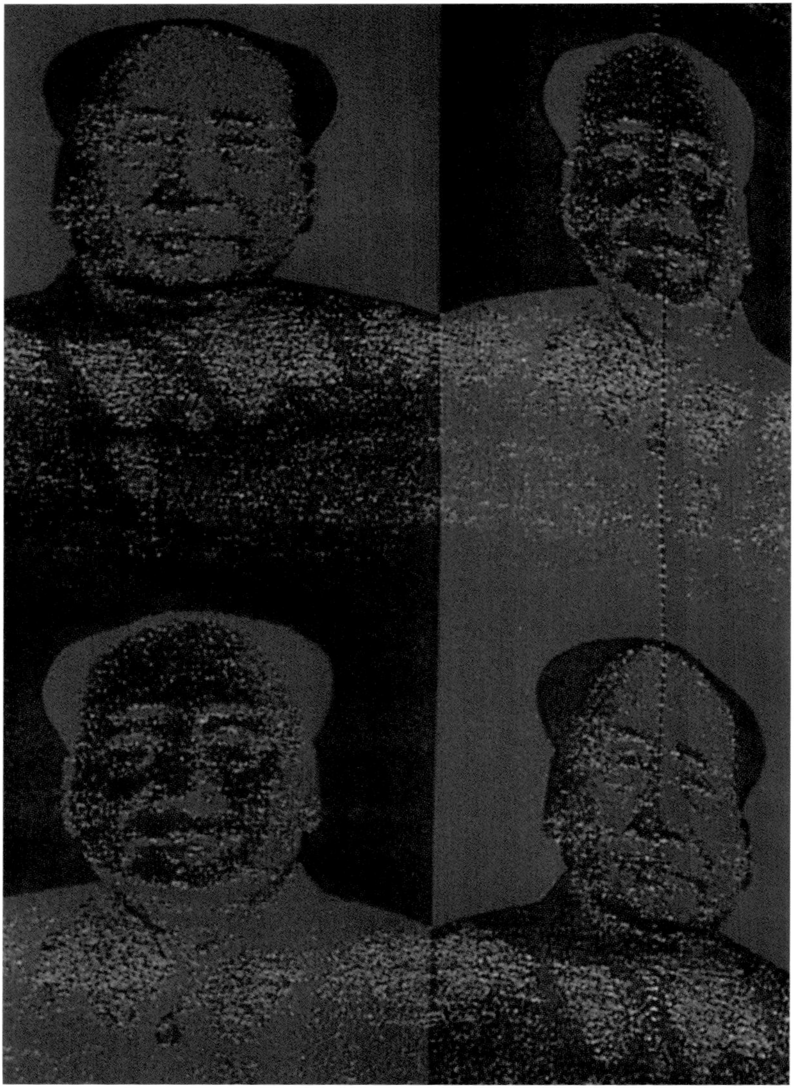

63
Vivienne Tam
Coat, polyester. Hong Kong, 1995 (V&A: FE.43–1998)

64
Vivienne Tam
Dress, nylon mesh. Hong Kong, 1995 (V&A: FE.44:1–1998)

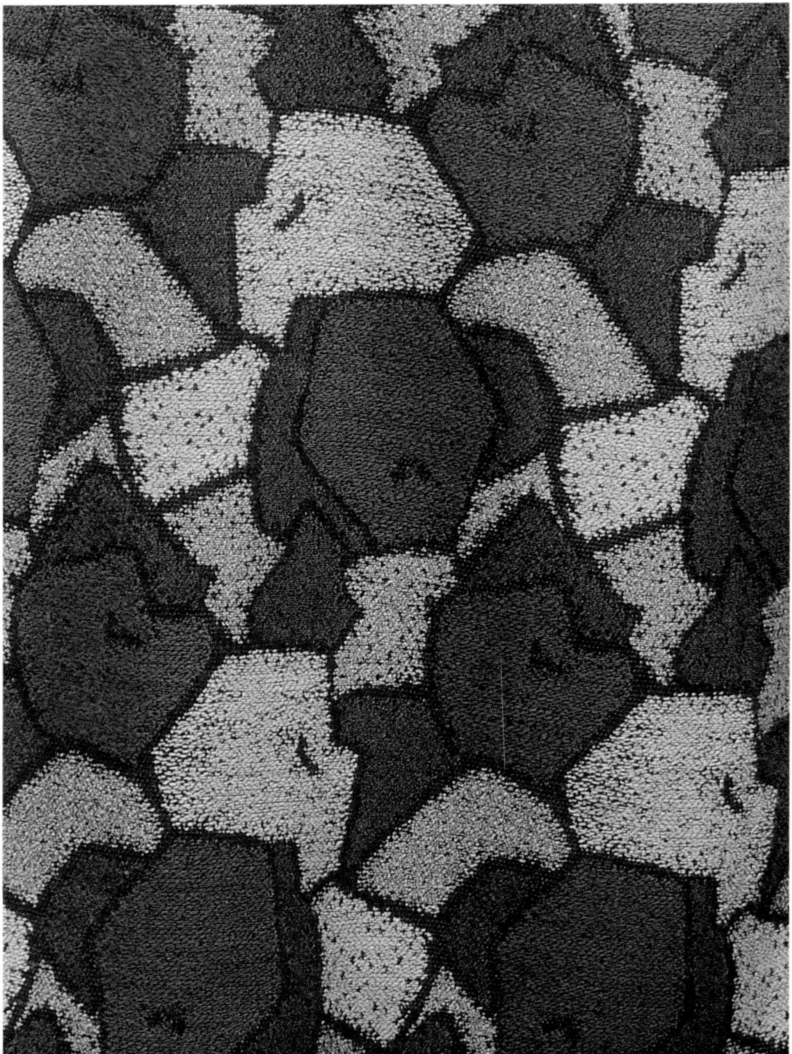

65
Qipao, woven rayon
Hong Kong, 1960–70 (V&A: FE.45–1995, Garrett Collection, Purchased with the support of the Friends of the V&A)

66
Qipao, silk chiffon
Hong Kong, 1940s (V&A: FE.42–1995, Garrett Collection, Purchased with the support of the Friends of the V&A)

Further Reading

Gao Hanyu
Chinese Textile Designs
London, 1992

Wong Hwei-Lian and Szan Tan, eds.
Power Dressing: Textiles for Rulers and Priests from the Chris Hall Collection
Singapore, 2006

Angelika Taschen, ed.
China Style
London, 2006

Ming Wilson, ed.
Imperial Chinese Robes
London, 2010

Verity Wilson
Chinese Dress
London, 1990

Verity Wilson
Chinese Textiles
London, 2005

Digital Images

The patterns reproduced in this book are stored on the accompanying compact disc as jpeg files (at approximately A5-size, 300 dpi). You should be able to open them, and manipulate them, direct from the CD-ROM in most modern image software (on Windows or Mac platforms), and no installation should be required (although we, as publishers, cannot guarantee absolutely that the disk will be accessible for every computer).

Instructions for tracing and tiling the images will be found with the documentation for your software.

The names of the files correspond to the V&A inventory numbers of the images.

Copyright